W9-CDL-767

Winnie the Pooh
ROO'S BIG NATURE DAY

By K. Emily Hutta

Illustrated by
Carson Van Osten, John Kurtz
& the Disney Storybook Artists

Some days are just quieter than others. Of course, there's nothing at all wrong with a quiet day—unless you're a roo of a rather youngish age. In that case, a quiet moment, or maybe two, is quite quiet enough.

"I'm *bored*!" Roo said, louder than was really necessary. "There's nothing to do around here!"

"I could read to you," Kanga said.

"I don't want to read," said Roo.

"We could bake something," Kanga suggested.

"It's too hot to bake," Roo complained.

"Do you want to do a puzzle?" asked Kanga.

"I've already done all of our puzzles," whined Roo.

3

"Why don't you go outside and find something to do?" Kanga said, gently nudging Roo toward the door.

"But I don't want . . ."

"I suppose I could find something useful for you to do inside," Kanga said. "You could help me shell peas. And then maybe clean up your room . . ."

Roo decided to go outside.

"There's nothing to do out here either!" Roo called over his shoulder.
Then it was quiet. Kanga let out a huge sigh of relief.
Suddenly Roo bounced into view outside the window. "I'm bored!"
he shouted.
"I'm still bored!" he yelled on the next bounce.

Just then, Tigger arrived and started bouncing next to Roo.

"What are we doing, Roo Boy?" Tigger asked.

"Nothing," Roo said.

"Nothing sure makes a tigger hot and tired," Tigger observed.

"Actually," Tigger said, "if I rememberate correctly, I was hot even before I started helping you bounce. In fact, I was on my way to the stream. Want to come along?"

"Can I go with Tigger to the stream?" Roo shouted to Kanga on his next three bounces up to the window.

"Oh! Yes! What a good idea!" Kanga said. And if she sounded exceptionally enthusiastic, well, perhaps it was not really all that difficult to understand why.

Roo and Tigger passed Rabbit's house on the way to the stream. Rabbit was leaning on a rake in his garden, looking sweaty and cross.

"We're going to the stream, Rabbit!" Roo announced.

"Why don't you come with us, Long Ears?" Tigger suggested. "It might be cooler there."

As they walked, the friends picked up more friends. Soon Eeyore, Owl, and Pooh had joined Tigger, Rabbit, and Roo.

"Halloooo," called a friendly little voice. "Where are you all off to?"

"Oh, look, it's Piglet," said Pooh happily. "We're going to the stream, Piglet. Won't you join us?"

"Oh, that would be splendid," said Piglet, running inside to get his hat.

When they got to the stream, everyone settled in the shade of a big tree.
"There's nothing to do around here," Roo said.
"We could eat," Pooh said hopefully. "Did anyone happen to bring any honey?"
No one had.

"How about a game?" Owl asked. "Did anyone bring a game to play?"

"No," said Rabbit, who was starting to look sweaty and cross all over again.

"That's just what I was afraid of," Eeyore said glumly. "No one brought anything useful at all."

"I brought my hat," Piglet said proudly.

"Well, there is that, I suppose," Eeyore said.

Piglet, who had been wise enough to bring his own shade, took a stroll along the stream. It was then that he made a truly wonderful discovery.

"Look at all of these smooth rocks!" Piglet called to his friends. "I haven't counted them, but I am absolutely certain that there are a very great number."

"But what can we do with them?" asked Roo.

"They look to me to be just the right configuration for rock-skipping," Owl said, coming to peer at the rocks.

"Well, I don't know about confingeratations, but I do know about skipping. And rock-skipping is what tiggers do best!" Tigger said.

"Actually, rock-skipping is one of the many things that *rabbits* do best," Rabbit said, and he sent a rock skipping across the water.

"Oh! Can you teach me to do that?" Roo asked excitedly.

So Rabbit gave his friends rock-skipping lessons and watched proudly as they tried out their new skills.

Piglet's tiny little rock danced lightly across the surface of the water.

Pooh's big round rock galumphed down to the bottom of the stream without a single skip—which was fine with Pooh because the splash was really very refreshing.

Tigger's best throw skipped three times—all of them on land.

And Roo . . . well, Roo was soon involved in a spirited rock-skipping contest with Rabbit, which ended in a tie.

Owl never threw his rocks at all. He meant to, but every time he picked one up, something about it caught his eye. Soon he was busy collecting rocks of every size and color and shape. Some had sparkles; some had swirls; some had bumpy, rough patches; and some were as smooth as glass. And when Owl wet his rocks in the stream, their colors and patterns got even brighter.

"Fascinating," Owl murmured. "Absolutely fascinating."

"I brought you some more rocks, Owl," said Eeyore. But he put them down too close to the edge of the stream, and they all slipped into the water.

"Oh, bother," Eeyore said sadly.

"No, look! Your rocks have made a little waterfall, Eeyore!" Owl said.

"It's splendid, Eeyore," Piglet said.

"What? What's going on?" asked Rabbit.

"Eeyore built a waterfall," Piglet said.

"I want to build a waterfall, too!" Roo announced. "Can you show me how, Eeyore?"

And so it happened that Eeyore—who was rarely asked for advice and had never before been listened to when he tried to offer any—found himself directing the waterfall-building effort.

Even Rabbit consulted him about how to keep his rocks from rolling down the stream. "It has been my experience," Eeyore said importantly, "that if you drop all of your rocks by accident into the water at precisely the same time, they will bunch up together in just the right waterfallish way."

By and by, a little puff of wind blew a leaf into the stream right next to Roo. Instead of sinking like a rock, the leaf floated—just like a boat!

Roo chased the leaf boat as it picked up speed, hurtled over several splendid waterfalls, and sailed out of sight!

"Did you see that? Did you see?" Roo shouted. "Who wants to sail leaf boats down the stream with me?"

As it happened, everyone did.

Rabbit was looking for more leaves to float when he made quite another discovery.

"What's that on your nose, Rabbit?" Pooh asked politely. It was important for a bear to be polite even when discussing things that might or might not be poking straight up off the top of someone else's nose.

"It's a pod," Rabbit said. "I found it under the tree."

"I want to wear a pod on my nose, too!" said Roo.

Soon all the friends were wearing pods on their noses—except Tigger, who had learned that pods and bouncing just don't mix.

But mud and bouncing—that was quite another matter. When a tigger happened to bounce into a mud patch, all sorts of satisfactory things happened. Squishy and squelchy things. Things that went *splat* and *splop* and *splatter*.

"Hey!" Roo shouted, wiping little gobs of mud from his front. "What do you think you're doing, Tigger?"

"No thinking," Tigger said. "Just doing!" And he bounced again, sending mud flying everywhere.

"I bet I can make the mud fly farther than you can!" Roo said, catapulting himself into the middle of the mud patch.

When all the bouncing and toe-squishing and mud-pie–making was done, Tigger and Roo were covered from head to foot in mud!

And that is why it took not just one, not even two, but three dunkings in the stream to get Roo and Tigger clean.

Afterward, Tigger and Roo stretched out in the late afternoon sun to dry.

Owl and Rabbit had their heads together, sorting Owl's new rock collection.

Pooh, who had explained to everyone who would listen that he never napped, was snoring softly in the shade.

Roo leaned over and tickled Pooh with a long blade of grass.

"Snorkelforkel," Pooh said, twitching his nose and rolling over.

Piglet was on his belly staring dreamily into a quiet pool, watching the reflections of the clouds drift by.

"In my experience," said Eeyore, "I've never looked so good."

Kanga stood, smiling to herself, enjoying the peaceful scene for a moment before she called out to Roo. "Time to go, dear."

"Oh, I don't want to leave!" Roo protested. "I'm having too much fun! Can I come again tomorrow?" he asked. "Can I?"

Kanga nodded.

"Yahoo! I can't wait!" Roo shouted, somewhat more loudly than was really necessary. *"There's so much to do around here!"*

Imagination

There's no such thing as "nothing to do,"
When nature is outside waiting for you.
The world is bursting with wonder and fun,
All it takes is your imagination.

Friends to the Rescue

Some days can be kind of bland,
For reasons we don't understand.
And so we droop and slump along,
Not knowing how to fix what's wrong.
No activity's appealing,
While we have that ho-hum feeling.

Then friends arrive and ring the bell,
And just like magic—all is well!
Oh, how wonderful life can be
(When instead of *I*, there is a *we*).

Nature Activity

In "Roo's Big Nature Day," Roo and his friends spend a long summer afternoon playing outside without a single toy or game. They use their imaginations to think of interesting ways to have fun with things from nature. They make boats from leaves and build waterfalls with rocks. They decorate their noses with pods and tickle Pooh's nose with grass. They play in the mud and skip stones in the stream. They stare into puddles and wonder at the shapes of the clouds.

And on this particular sunny day, Owl starts a rock collection. He notices for the first time how every rock is different and special. He sees the sparkles and swirls and colors that you only really see if you take the time to look closely. He and Rabbit discover that it's fun and fascinating to sort the rocks by size and shape and color.

The wonderful thing about rocks is that you can find them everywhere! Next time you're outside, be on the lookout for rocks of different colors, sizes, and shapes. You can wet them and see how much brighter the colors become. You can build things with them—such as Eeyore's waterfall or a pyramid or a wall. You can even start your own rock collection—just like Owl!

At Kohl's, we believe the simple act of caring creates a sense of community. Thanks to people like you, over the past 10 years Kohl's Cares for Kids ® has raised millions of dollars to support children in the communities we serve. Throughout the year, Kohl's sells special Kohl's Cares for Kids merchandise with 100% percent of the net profit benefiting children's health and education initiatives nationwide.

Kohl's Cares for Kids is our way of supporting our customers and improving children's lives. So when you turn the pages of this book, remember you're not only reading a fun-filled adventure, you're also helping make a difference in the life of a child.

For more information about Kohl's Cares for Kids programs, visit www.kohlscorporation.com.

SUSTAINABLE FORESTRY INITIATIVE

Certified Fiber Sourcing

www.sfiprogram.org

PWC-SFICOC-260
FOR TEXT PAPER ONLY

For more Disney Press fun, visit www.disneybooks.com